MASTERING PROJECT MANAGEMENT